PRAY IT NOW

Prayers for Everyone

By
Barry & Valerie Moore

Pray It Now
Prayers for Everyone
Authored by Barry & Valerie Moore
© Barry & Valerie Moore 2022
Edited and proofread by Lee Dickinson Published by Marcia M Spence of Marcia M Publishing House, West Bromwich, West Midlands the UNITED KINGDOM B71 on behalf of the authors.
Cover and interior design Marcia M Publishing House.

ISBN: 9781913905347

www.marciampublishing.com

Praise for Prayers

Good Morning Barry and Valerie,
Amen and thank you for these powerful and timely words of
encouragement concerning prayer.
God bless you both, for this amazing ministry. **MW**

Amen and thank you for the Valuable Words of Truth. Every
blessing to you and your family.
Gwen Nelson

Amen. Let's keep prayerful always. **A.D G**

Thank you, Sis/Pastor, this is good.
Praise the Lord for His favour to me, thank God for sending me
this prayer through you. Truly the Lord looks after His own.
Thank God for you and for this powerful prayer hallelujah!
Maurcia Mitchell

Hi Barry and Valerie,

God bless you for your ministry you are a great support, and these prayers are always anointed so I thank you greatly. **Rev T R Hatton**

NTCG Beeston Leeds

DEDICATIONS

This book is dedicated to:

Jehovah God, our Father in heaven, for inspiration, guidance and revelation, to write and send His Word to the world.

Jane Elizabeth and Wilford Alexander Cunningham ~ Mum and Dad who taught me to pray. Valerie

Nathan Heath ~ my Grandfather who gave me his Bible to read and brought me up to be a man. Barry

CONTENTS

FOREWORD

By Rev Adrian Cox

When Val, and Barry, whom I call my spiritual son, approached me to write a foreword for this book, I accepted with joy, as I know and admire these wonderful, humble, sincere and anointed servants of God. I am reminded of how the Apostle Paul said he felt joyful every time he prayed for the church in Philippi; I also am filled with joy as I write this foreword.

God brought this wonderful couple into our life when they became members of the New Testament Church of God in Huddersfield, and as they yielded themselves to God, He used them as His instruments for the edifying of His church.

I was the adult Bible class teacher, and there was a need for an assistant. We, the leadership of the church, perceived that there was a special calling upon my brother's life, and when he was approached and asked, he obeyed the heavenly call and the church was made richer through the preached word as presented by both Barry and Val. With the skills, wisdom and God's anointing, God used Val in the education department of our church, which reached new heights. It brings joy to my heart when I look back on Barry and Val Moore, as they were not only a blessing to the church, but God also brought them into a special relationship with my family.

I am one who has been blessed with countless others across the globe by the very successful daily PrayItNow Ministries prayer ministry that God inspired Barry and Val to launch. I know Barry and Val are a man and woman of God, well-versed in God's Word, and guided by the Holy Spirit.

I have no doubt that anyone reading this book will be blessed and inspired to live the overcoming Christian life.

ACKNOWLEDGEMENTS

"And I thank Christ Jesus our Lord, who hath enabled me, for that he counted me faithful, putting me into ministry;" (1 Tim 1:12).

We give immeasurable honour to God our Father, our Lord Jesus Christ and the person of the Holy Spirit, who have inspired the writing of this book for the spreading of the gospel of Jesus Christ. "According to the glorious gospel of the blessed God, which was committed to my trust." (1 Tim 1:11).

Pastor David Perrin, many years ago you asked if we had thought about putting our prayers into a book. Well, Here it is!

During the past ten years, God has placed a good few hundred faithful people, family, friends, brethren and neighbours who have walked alongside us: sharing our prayers and encouragements across the world; many of you who in writing to us daily have been a great source of ongoing encouragement. To every person who has sent us a prayer request, you have helped us focus on our love of prayer. To everyone who phoned/wrote and shared your testimonies of answered prayers, shared how our prayers impact your lives, checked on our wellbeing, sent us your encouragement and prayers to keep going and thanked us for the ministry, our commitment and faithfulness, may heaven bless you all.

In 2021 we shared our aspirations to publish a book of prayer with Jerome Williams. He encouraged us to publish, advised on the book layout, sharing it with the widest audience and creating what he thought might be best impact. Jerome acknowledged that our prayers touched many areas of everyday life such as: personal/self-development, family and community. This flows with feedback from many people over the past ten years. In Jerome's testimony, we see an example of our prayers inspiring life changes. Jerome, we thank you for your time, encouragement, advice and support regarding our book project.

Paulette Haye-Allen, you never missed a single morning. Without realising it, you became our early warning system. If a prayer/encouragement was late, you sent us a WhatsApp or text to find out where it was…
We thank everyone at Marcia M Publishing House and Academy for their love, guidance and support along this publishing journey.

Many thanks go out to Lee for the 'thorough edit' and our learning experience.

The Lord bless you all!

We remember:
Mrs Agatha Laing
Miss Colleen Laing
Rev Jasmine Comrie

They are no longer here with us but in their own way, they each encouraged us to continue with this ministry of prayer. We remember them with love in Christ.

INTRODUCTION

to This Book of Prayer

Our inspiration for writing this book and what propels us is to share the gospel of Jesus Christ with the world (Mt 28) in love through the Holy Spirit. We are now celebrating ten years of writing and sending out daily prayers and encouragement through PrayItNow Ministries. It is a blessing to encourage people to accept that they are loved by Jehovah God and know that He cares about them, their families and communities, their fears, hopes and dreams. God does not want a single person to worry or give up on life (Jn 3:16).

We have collated a selection of inspired prayers in one place, which themselves, in part, testify of our own journey of faith, our love of prayer and God equipping us for ministry. We pressed along as the Lord sustained us, answering our prayers and motivating us when we were physically exhausted. We take all our challenges to the Lord and He works them out. It is truly amazing how sufficient God's grace is when you recognise that it is God's grace that keeps you – not your own strength.

The prayers in this book will inspire you to pray and can be prayed by anyone, Christian or non-Christian. They will equip you to pray the Scriptures with confidence, fulfil God's commandment to pray, and never give up (1 Tm 2:1-4; 1 Thes 5:17; Lk 18:1; Col 4:2; Eph 1:15-16) and strengthen your faith in God's Word.

We encourage you to answer the call to pray, be unafraid and unashamed to pray. See prayer as an unbreakable lifeline in your relationship with God. "For all who are led by God's Spirit are God's children" (Rom 8:14, read vs 15-16, ISV). The prayers and encouragements will lead you to recognise that we are at war in the spirit (Eph 6:12). The prayers will strengthen you to stand against and disrupt the plans of the enemy through spiritual warfare.

Pray for yourself and others who need an intercessor. Adapt the prayers as needed with the Holy Spirit's help.

HOW PRAYITNOW
Ministries Came to Be Started

Ps 71:16-18

To Edify, Strengthen and Encourage Prayer

PrayItNow Ministries was started in 2011 to spread the gospel and to encourage the saints daily to continue to pray. It was started when I was at a low place in terms of my health and as I wanted to continue to minister. I had numerous hospital appointments, for X-rays and MRI scans to investigate the small cyst found on my spinal cord. I was told it was in a dangerous place to operate. I recall seeing one specialist who saw my scan and told me I should not have the ability to walk and should not have any feelings below my waist. He then set out to prove it by trying to break my knee with his hammer (not literally, of course). When I told him he was hurting me, he looked at me in disbelief and continued hitting my knee. This was when my wife stepped in to communicate the fact that, if I said he was hurting, then he was.

My back prevented me from going out to work. At times I was unable to assist my wife around the house and spent hours lying in bed. Many Sundays I was in bed unable to attend the house of the Lord where I worshipped and served in many different capacities: preaching, teaching adult Sunday school, men's ministry, prayer ministry, health and safety team, prison ministry, BtG, and street pastors.

One Sunday while lying in bed, I asked the Lord where in the ministry he would use me. As I lay in the silence the Lord spoke: your ministry is in your phone. At first I did not understand, but it soon became clear that my contacts were to be the beginning of the prayer ministry. I had initially started sending out prayers and encouragements by email, but had no idea how the ministry would grow. Valerie and I wrote a 'welcome to the ministry' note, and it began with 'welcome to the mobile phone prayer ministry', which was sent to everyone we added to our list. I started sending WhatsApps to seven people; this number grew to between 300 and 400 including emails and texts. I bless God that these prayers and encouragements, sent daily, have reached many places across the world.

Barry Moore

JEROME'S TESTIMONY

As a Christian, I believe that prayer and the power of prayer can bring about healing. Through the meaningful power of prayers the healing will come. Healing may come gradually, and that means the particular affliction is being used for God's glory, for the development of character or maybe as a sermon. Some of the prayers I received over the years are maintained in a database and, in recent times, I forwarded some to a neighbour who wanted to help a son experiencing a severe reversal in fortunes. He was a constant drug abuser, turned his back on his young family, and lost all hope of living. He became suicidal and was found in his home passed out from gas poisoning. The family were former Christians but, in their words, "turned their backs against any form of worshipping".

Some six months later, the family approached me and thanked me for the prayers. They found that the nature and use of the prayers brought a sense of calmness and tranquillity, and they felt better prepared to deal with problems their son experienced. They felt they had the strength and strategy to clearly think their way through the difficulties they faced. So how you feel about prayers and what prayers mean to you is essential. If you approach prayers in that way, there is every chance they will bring comfort to you.

Written by Jerome Williams 2022

Pray It Now
Prayers for Everyone

By Barry & Valerie Moore

CHAPTER 1

A Call to Prayer – But Why on Earth Should You Pray?

Introduction

What Is a Prayer?

P rayer is the way we, as Christian believers, communicate with Jehovah God our Father in heaven. Prayer is central to developing an intimate relationship with God. It is the primary means by which we express our thoughts and feelings with God – who can do all things. We acknowledge God for who He is, worship, give thanks and make requests. An effective prayer is one prayed from the heart. Bartimaeus prayed out loud: "Jesus, thou Son of David, have mercy on me" (Mk 20:47). Hallelujah! Prayer is the ultimate weapon in spiritual warfare.

Why You Must Pray

God who answers prayers has commanded that you pray. He calls you to pray in Lk 18:1, Lk 21:36, Col 4:2, 1 Tm 2:1-4 and many other scriptures. Jesus prayed continually to the Father and, as his followers, we must also pray. When we sin against God, we make things right by praying for forgiveness, confess our sin, say sorry and ask God to forgive us. God will hear our prayers from wherever we are. Jonah prayed in the belly of a fish.

Making Requests to God

Read 1 Tm 2:1-4 – who to pray for; Jas 5:13-16 – things to pray for; and Jas 5:17-18 – one of Elijah's powerful prayers.

Prayers for You, and for Other People

You can pray these prayers for yourself, for family, friends, brethren and neighbours near and far. Pray from a heart filled with love and compassion.

Lord, Let Me Be My Best

Lord, today I bless your name with renewed vigour. I thank you and bless you for waking me up this morning and I ask you to fill me up with all the benefits I need for today as I go. Let me be the best that I can be in Christ, doing my best at work, ministering goodness in my attitude to people. Father, in Jesus' name, season me with salt so that my conversations will be seasoned, and my walk upright in every step glorifying your name. In Jesus' name. Amen.

Encouragement to Pray – Prayer Awakens Us

We pray to God the Father, through Jesus Christ for peace, for healing, advances in science against cancer, strength and wisdom to eradicate poverty and disease, the courage to stand against and overcome injustice, for resolve, for others, for ourselves and our children. Pray to God in the Spirit with all your heart and soul, and then gather up your might to meet the challenges that lie ahead. Pray against brokenness, broken marriages and broken relationships.

Pray for a deeper relationship with our God, for reconciliation and restoration. We pray for those who suffer loss and for bereaved families. Pray in Jesus' name: there is power in His name. Prayer is not a passive activity. It changes us. It awakens us. Our eyes begin to notice beauty where we never noticed it before. Our hearts begin to feel compassion that we never knew we had. Our priorities shift. And as we talk to God, we receive the encouragement and strength to live up to the potential He has put inside us. Soon we start to see beyond ourselves into the world that is waiting for our help; waiting to hear the gospel of Jesus Christ that they might live. Hallelujah!

May God bless you in this new day as you pray in Jesus' name. Amen.

A Prayer for Blessings

Eternal and everlasting Father in heaven, hallowed be thy holy name. I thank you Lord for making a way for us all to come into your presence, make requests, intercede, make supplication, confess and praise your most holy name. Father, thank you. Father, I pray your words this day for blessings on the person praying this prayer, in Jesus' name. Amen.

"Be anxious for nothing, but in everything by prayer and supplication, with thanksgiving, let your requests be made known to God" (Phil 4:6). "Call to me, and I will answer thee, and shew thee great and mighty things, which thou knowest not" (Jer 33:3). "Behold, I am the Lord, the God of all flesh. Is there anything too hard for me?" (Jer 32:27). Lord, I believe that all things are possible with you and I am trusting you to lead me into a closer relationship with you, in Jesus' name. Amen.

Your Word says, "Come to me, all you who are troubled and weighted down with care, and I will give you rest" (Mt 11:28, BBE). So Lord, I ask you to help me, to help my family and other people to come to you so that they might be saved and know that you will never leave nor forsake them. (Heb 13:5). The book of Ephesians tells me of your blessings, "Blessed be the God and Father of our Lord Jesus Christ, who has blessed us with every spiritual blessing in the heavenly places in Christ" (Eph 1:3), for which I'm thankful, and I ask for the full blessings of your Word to become real in my life as I give you thanks, in the name of Jesus Christ, Amen.

Lift Your Faith

In the book of Hebrews, some of the things we learn about include faith, acts of faith, great faith and outcomes of faith. Heb 11:1 says: "Now faith is the substance of things hoped for, the evidence of things not seen". Rom 1:17 tells us: "The just shall live by faith". When we believe God, we will trust Him to do what is right for us; we won't spend our time trying to sort things out ourselves. Almighty God made us all to be His glory from the smallest child to the greatest adult. In fact, every kind of person who will believe Him and put their faith in Him.

God's Word tells us that He looks out for us; He has good plans for us, that He will never leave nor forsake us or leave us comfortless. When we have faith in God, we will be obedient to His will and keep his commandments. Our faith enables us to act on what we don't see as a reality. The Bible is filled with stories of faith, including how Abraham's faith took him on a journey of belief, trust and discovery. The outcome was he reached and inherited the land God had promised him.

If you believe Jn 14:2-3, then believe that Jesus is able to take care of you in the here and now. Put your faith in Jesus and be faithful to Him, because He is always faithful. When you pray, ask 'our Father' to increase your faith, for the righteous individual lives by a strong belief in God and knowledge of who God is. Amen.

Pray Together

There is a name that moves obstacles, lifts heavy loads, heals bodies – physically and mentally. That name is Jesus. When we pray in His name, He increases our faith, opens doors when we knock, and He gives when we ask according to His will. Now let's pray in the name of Jesus:

Dear heavenly Father God, we thank you for this new day. We thank you for all the good things that you have done and continue to do in our lives each day: new insights, revelations, warmth and love. We thank you that when we didn't know each other, you brought us together as a family, your family, through Jesus Christ.

Father, we thank you because you loved us so much, you gave your only son, Jesus, to die in our place on a cross at Calvary. We thank you that even though we don't deserve all the good things you do for us, you keep doing them, like waking us up each morning, giving us the right words to speak to strangers who don't know you. Thank you Lord. Amen.

Father, in the name of your son Jesus, we ask you to hear all our prayers today and answer us right soon so that we can do right and be in right standing with you. Father, in the name of Jesus, we pray for all our children and families to be healed, set free, from every type of trick, trap, enticement, deception, addiction, accident, trips and falls. In the name of Jesus, cause us all to repent for the things we have done wrong, Lord, and save us from all our sins in Jesus' name. Amen.

Prayer for Your Peace and Comfort

May the everlasting peace of God surround you and comfort you, and His arm defend you. I pray that the troubles of this present time never overcome you. I pray no fire touch you, nor waters overflow you. I pray the valley of the shadow of death will not cause you to fear, because your God loves you. No weapon formed against you shall prosper. I pray that your defence will hear you and answer you accordingly, as He has promised. I pray that God, your God, would hide you in His secret place, and that He would cover you with His wings. I pray that God would turn up on time, in time for your situations, because He is a timely God. Father in heaven, prepare a table before my brethren that they may be satisfied; a table with every need supplied, where every evil plan is broken.

O God, break the bands of wickedness from us in the name of Jesus: from over our children, from over our church, from over our communities. I declare this over the whole world. Hallelujah! Bring your people to you, O God, for your glory and for your praise. Hallelujah! Hallelujah! I ask you, Lord, in no other name but the name of our Lord Jesus Christ. "Neither is there salvation in any other: for there is none other name under heaven given among men, whereby we must be saved" (Acts 4:12). Lord, I ask for favour for all your people in the name of Jesus, giving you all the glory and all the praise. Amen.

A Prayer for Faith

Dear heavenly Father of life, who comforts the faithful, we pray that you would grant your servants faith like the men and women of old, who through faith subdued kingdoms, wrought righteousness, obtained promises, stopped the mouths of lions (Heb 11:33), like Daniel who said, "My God has sent his angel to keep the lions' mouths shut, and they have done me no damage: because I was seen to be without sin before him; and further, before you, O King, I have done no wrong" (Dan 6:22, BBE). Like the saints who (Heb 11:34) "quenched the violence of fire, escaped the edge of the sword, out of weakness were made strong, waxed valiant in fight, turned to flight the armies of the aliens".

In the name of Jesus Christ, Lord we pray that through your grace, we will serve you faithfully from this day forward believing your Word in Heb 11:6, which states: "Now without faith it is impossible to please God, for whoever comes to him must believe that he exists and that he rewards those who diligently search for him" (ISV). Father, increase our faith and heal our unbelief so that, like the saints of old, we will serve and please you faithfully, in Jesus' name. Thank you Father. Amen.

Jehovah Bless You

I pray that, God, our Great and Gracious Jehovah, will bless you, and that his keeping power will keep you, and the glory of his face would shine upon you, and our God, the God of peace, would overflow you in abundance with peace, the peace of God that passes all understanding. I pray in Jesus' name that the still waters where he leads us will refresh you, body and soul. Father, forgive us, draw us close to you and cover, hide, shelter your people. Be with us Lord, as you promised you would be with us in times of trouble, for all of us, for our little ones, our friends, brothers, sisters, wives, husbands, mothers and fathers, all of the family. May every work of the enemy be broken and brought to nothing, in Jesus' name. Thank you Lord, Amen.

Faith to Pray

The spiritual gift of faith is exhibited by those with a strong and unshakeable confidence in God, His Word, His promises, and the power of prayer to bring about miracles. I pray that God would anoint you with a gift of prayer. I pray that prayer would pour out of you, out of the good treasure of your heart. I pray that your mind would be stayed on Christ. I pray that nothing but the power of the Holy Spirit would move, direct and inspire you. I pray the Holy Spirit of God's protection over you, in Jesus' name. I pray that you would pray to our Father in every kind of circumstance, in every situation without prejudice, in the mighty name of Jesus Christ. Hallelujah! Amen.

God Is Faithful

"For I reckon that the sufferings of this present time are not worthy to be compared with the glory which shall be revealed in us" (Rom 8:18). "For our light affliction, which is but for a moment, worketh for us a far more exceeding and eternal weight of glory" (2 Cor 4:17). "There hath no temptation taken you but such as is common to man: but God is faithful, who will not suffer you to be tempted above that ye are able; but will with the temptation also make a way to escape, that ye may be able to bear it" (1 Cor 10:13). Rom 8:28 says all things work together for good to them that love the Lord.

I pray that every suffering, and every affliction, works for good for you to bring glory to God. In the name of Jesus Christ, Amen.

CHAPTER 2

Relationships

Introduction

Jn 3:16 tells us, "For God so loved the world, that he gave his one and only Son, that whoever believes in him should not perish, but have eternal life" (WEB).

As Peter tells us, Jesus died for everyone: an innocent person for every guilty person so that he could bring us back to God (1 Pt 3:18). This is the greatest sacrifice that anyone could make for another person. Through the death and resurrection of Jesus Christ, everyone can have a relationship with God. This is exactly what God wants for us: to be reconciled to Him and be in right standing with Him in a righteous relationship. This describes the most powerful relationship that any person can have as there is no failure in God. So, irrespective of whether a person believes that God exists or not, God's unconditional love is already given. God also wants us to be reconciled one with another. Fervent, effectual prayer can change relationship issues in: families, workspaces, congregations, schools, colleges and governments. Pray and build strong, godly relationships.

Prayer for All Relationships

Lord God of heaven, keep us, O Lord, from pettiness, childishness and spitefulness. Let us be thoughtful in word and deed. Help us to put away falseness, pretence and face each other in deep trust without fear or self-pity, being honest and sincere.

Help us to guard against fault-finding, criticism, and the lies of complaint and be quick to discover the best in each other in every circumstance, and situation. Guard us from ill temper and hasty judgements; encourage us to take time for all our relationships, to grow calm, serene and gentle. Help us to be generous with kind encouraging words and compliments. Teach us never to ignore, never to hurt and never to take each other for granted. Engrave charity and compassion on our hearts, in the mighty peace-giving name of our Lord and Saviour Jesus Christ. Thank you Lord. Amen.

Holy Spirit Cover for Families

I pray the Spirit of the Lord God and the life-giving blood of Jesus Christ over our children. Holy Spirit, turn them and detain them. Wash over their souls, Father, in Jesus' holy name. Hallelujah! I pray for our work: may God bless prosper and multiply the works of our hands by the power of the Holy Spirit. By the power of the Holy Spirit watch over wives and husbands. Let not that which you have ordained be corrupted, but rebuke the hand of evil from every marriage in Jesus' name. Hallelujah! Hallelujah! Hallelujah! For the leaders and ministers in the body of Christ, Father, in Jesus' name by the power of the Holy Spirit, cover them as with a blanket of protection, Father. Do no less for world leaders; fall on them, spirit of the true and living God, in Jesus' name. Thank you, Father, for the power of the Holy Spirit. Amen.

As a Father

Father, blessed be thy name, in Jesus' name. Lord, as a man I thank you for who I am to you. Sometimes, Lord, as a father it is difficult to deal with the waywardness of our children who are drawn to the things of the world. Sometimes it feels like a steep uphill struggle to train them up, Lord, as you have asked, but then, Lord, I often ask myself who can be a father like you; we so often allow things to slip. In Jesus' name, I want to be the father you want me to be, so teach me, Lord. I am asking in Jesus' name that you would furnish me with the right spiritual conversation, that I may call to their souls not just my own children but to the children of the world, in Jesus' name. Amen.

Prayer For Our Elders

Father, in the name of Jesus Christ our everlasting Saviour, I give you thanks and praise for all our mothers, fathers, grandparents, elders, aunts and uncles. Father, I ask in no other name but the name of Jesus Christ, that you surround them with your divine protection, mercies and grace and your tender loving care. Your Word instructs us to cast our cares on you because you care for us; I pray that your care would be multiplied to the weak in Jesus' name. Give strength to the weary, Lord, comfort the elderly as the years roll on, those who have suffered loss, healing for those suffering sickness, those in hospital, and at home – keep them sound.

Father, without our elders we would not be here and so Lord bless them with everlasting blessings. Lord Jesus, continue to walk with them and give them abundant peace, comfort those who are lonely. Refresh the weary. Be a shield Lord around them by the blood of Jesus Christ, and may your Holy Spirit dwell with and give long life to our mothers, fathers, grandfathers and grandmothers – all our elders – as we recognise them and give you thanks for every blessing, in the mighty name of Jesus Christ. Amen.

As a Single Mother

Lord, I come to you as a mother of children for advice on how to be the best that I can be to love them, nurture them, and be firm. But as a single mother, I often get so tired with the stress of bills, school, health, clothes, but, Lord, I know your Word says that you will supply all my needs according to your riches in glory. Lord, supply me with strength in my time of weakness to be who I must be. Lord, I ask you in Jesus' name, help me. Amen.

Prayer for Christian Men and Women

Loving, gracious, and everlasting Father, thank you for the man-child, Jesus Christ, our perfect example of a godly man, a man who demonstrated that godly living means to walk in your will, in spirit and in truth, totally surrendering to the Holy Spirit in obedience to you, our heavenly Father. Lord, in the name of Jesus Christ, I plead the life, blood and character of Jesus over the lives of Christian men and women everywhere. Lifting up holy hands, I lift up godly Christian men and women and pray that your spirit of grace and truth may rest, remain and abide with us all, through Jesus Christ. Amen.

I pray that Christian men and women may grow in grace and in the knowledge of Christ Jesus our Lord, that we may become strong in the power of His might, not relying on our own abilities but trusting in Jesus alone. May the beautiful character of the Lord Jesus be increasingly reflected in each one and may Christian men and women throughout the world be godly ambassadors of the truth of the gospel; and be kings, priests, and prophets both in our own homes, congregations, communities and all we come into contact with.

I pray that as men and women of God we would have a strong desire to love our wives and husbands, remembering how Christ loved the church and gave himself for it. Lord, build up men and women in the body of Christ. I pray for an army of Christian men and women: men and women of strength and integrity who will become a reflection of the Lord Jesus in every way, so that we may continue to grow into mighty men of valour – men of God, women of virtue and substance. In the mighty name of Jesus Christ, we give you thanks, Lord. Amen.

As a Husband

Blessed Saviour, glory to your name. Father, I know that you created the relationship of marriage. You ordained that it should be so and I have determined that as a husband I will fulfil my role in lifting up your name in it. Knit and bind me to my wife, Father, teach me how to communicate, and how to be gentle, respectful and loving that the pattern of my lifestyle will lead to positive outcomes in our relationship, in your kingdom, in Jesus' name. Amen.

For the Generations

Today, Lord, I come to you on behalf of our children and their children, our siblings, our relatives, aunts, uncles, grandparents, our sisters and brothers in Christ. Lord, I pray that you would overshadow them in all their movements, sleeping, waking, walking and talking. Bless their speaking and listening Lord and open their ears to hear what you are saying, what you are speaking directly into their spirit. I pray that you would bless us with the words spoken in Ez 11:19: "And I will give them one heart, and I will put a new spirit within you; and I will take the stony heart out of their flesh and will give them a heart of flesh". In the name of Jesus, I pray and give thanks. Amen.

Peace in Relationships

Eternal Everlasting God, I pray send peace for all families and relationships. Restore the love, joy and happiness, remove dark clouds of sadness and heal brokenness, in Jesus' name. Thank you Lord. Amen.

Forgive and Heal

Father, we magnify, glorify and lift up your name. Thank you for the strength of your Word to deliver, heal and redeem. Blessed be the name of the Most High God. Father, as you did with Daniel, cause us to look to your Word that we might understand the social, economic and political times that we live in, and that we might call on your name, seek your face; pray as Daniel prayed in Dn 9, turn from our sinful ways and receive your promise to heal our land.

Father, in the name of Jesus Christ, we pray that you would anoint and strengthen church leaders, ministers and members to be the examples that this world needs. Father, we pray for world leaders to receive new vision, insight, spiritual realisation and understanding of who you are; to see clearly and make right decisions for all the nations of this world. We ask that you intervene in the decision-making processes in the UK and all of Europe to bring equality to our communities and to call the people to live in peace. In Jesus' name we pray and say thank you Lord. Amen.

CHAPTER 3

Healing and Deliverance

Introduction

J as 5:14 says: "Is any sick among you? Let him call for the elders of the church; and let them pray over him, anointing him with oil in the name of the Lord."

Being a member of a Christian church gives you immediate access to prayer for healing. If you are not part of a church congregation, you can still request prayer for healing. Healing comes from God (Ex 15:26). He has power over all life. It is neither the person who prays or lays hands on you that brings about your healing; the anointing of the Holy Spirit does the work. Jas 5:15 tells us that the prayer of faith shall save the sick and if they have committed sin their sins shall be forgiven them. What a promise!

Christian believers of Christ Jesus are duty-bound to pray. Many families across the world have been touched or devastated by Covid. They need prayer for healing and deliverance along with the millions suffering from other sicknesses and torments. So, if you are sick or someone you know is sick, ask the church to pray for healing. Search the Bible for healing. You will find some examples as you journey through this book. Read and pray.

I Speak Life

I speak salvation for everyone who does not yet have a relationship with the Lord. Life for those waiting; may you gain strength. Life for those with life limiting illnesses, disabling conditions, afflictions, stress; may you receive your healing in the name of Jesus. God can heal; He is more than able to deliver. I declare life. It is in the power and authority of the tongue to command, and I command life, in Jesus' holy name. Amen.

A Prayer for Healing

Pray this prayer Out Loud with authority in the name of Jesus Christ:

Father in heaven, blessed be thy name, from the rising of the sun to the setting of the same. We praise you, not for what you do but for who you are; you are Almighty God. Today, in Jesus' name, I come against every curse, every sickness, high blood pressure, heart disease, diabetes, cancer, arthritis, sickness of the eyes, every unnamed sickness which affects your people, and I declare, Lord Jesus, that by your stripes we are healed, restored and reconciled. Today I push against every resistance and touch the hem of your garment on behalf of your people by faith. By your divine power, divine authority, and blood, I send your Word to heal and restore every soul and deliver out of every destructive situation this morning, in Jesus' name. You are the God that heals. Make haste, O God, to deliver. Arise O Lord God and scatter our enemies, in the name of Jesus Christ, I give you thanks. Amen.

A Prayer to Ease Pain

Father, I reach out to you today and ask for relief for those who are afflicted with headaches and migraines. Ease the tension in the muscles, blood vessels and nerves of their heads, necks and bodies. In Jesus' name, release peace in their bodies and let them sleep and recuperate. Heal their headaches now and stop chronic headaches, migraines, and pain from returning as we cast them back into the pit of hell from where they came. Father, I pray by faith that your healing power would be poured into and over the lives of those suffering with every type of chronic pain in the name of Jesus Christ. And in the name of Jesus Christ, Father, ease the pain that comes after surgery, pain of old injuries, of accidents, pain caused by emotional trauma, heartbreak, upset, and pain of loss. Father, I ask for your healing anointing to destroy emotional turmoil, its causes and its effects, in name of our Lord and Saviour Jesus Christ. Hallelujah! Lord, you are the Comforter; comfort those in pain, ease suffering and pour your peace into the minds and bodies of your people, as we pray in Jesus' holy name and give you thanks. Amen.

A Prayer to Break Addiction

Pray out loud over yourself and your family:

Everlasting Father, I surrender my life to you; please take total and absolute control of my body, soul, spirit and life. I give myself into your hand. Please cleanse me with the blood of Jesus Christ, in Jesus' name (1 Jn 1:7). Father, I come to you on behalf of every single individual that you have created and my request is that every addiction, everything that holds your people captive, be broken in the name of Jesus Christ. Father, break those things that we do that cause us to be ill, to be bound by the tricks and enticements of the enemy. Father, in Jesus' name arise, scatter the enemy, break the chains of bondage, of drugs, abuse, knife crime, gun crime from our children, from the church and our communities by the blood of Jesus Christ. Draw us close to you, walk with us, counsel us, lead us in the way that we should go and keep us free from all addiction in the mighty, everlasting, blood-cleansing name of Jesus Christ. I give you thanks, O God, Amen.

For Healing and Deliverance from Mental Ill Health

Dear gracious Father, I pray that by your everlasting unfathomable love, you would heal your people, your children and young people suffering with mental health problems. Please, bring relief to their troubled minds Lord, pour out your favour upon them, speak into their spirit and let them know deep down that you love and care for them, that you watch over them and that you can heal them. Lord, don't let your people suffer this evil from the depths of hell; it breaks hearts and tears families apart, it brings death, emptiness, pain, hurt, suffering and hopelessness. They cut themselves and they feel useless, unable to accept help and support, some just want to die. Father God, you are a God of love, so pour out your love, mercy and compassion, and let us see your miraculous healing in the lives of these sufferers. So, in the name of Jesus Christ of Nazareth, by faith, and by the unfailing, unquenchable power of the Holy Spirit, I declare healing and deliverance on everyone suffering mental ill health. And I give you all the glory and all the praise Father God, in Jesus' name. Amen.

The Blood – Declaration

Father in heaven, hallowed be your great name. At your name, O Lord, demons tremble and flee, in Jesus' name. Father, your Word says in 2 Cor 10:4: "For the weapons of our warfare are not carnal, but mighty through God to the pulling down of strong holds". In the name of Jesus Christ, be glorified, O God, as I come against every kind of spiritual stronghold, against powers and principalities. I plead the blood of Jesus Christ, by the power of the Holy Ghost, against spoken curses over our children and young people, over marriages, and relationships, and ask, O God, that you cover them under the shadow of your wings.

I pray for wisdom for your people, supernatural strength, and a discerning spirit to know what is right, in Jesus' name. I draw out the weapon of our warfare against lies, deception, trickery, accusing, complaining, and failure to make correction in the body of Christ – the church. I pray for resolutions to historical issues by the authority of the Holy Ghost. And I pray that anger, animosity, and backbiting would be shattered to pieces in the name of Jesus Christ. I pray for reconciliation, and healing in abundance for absent family members; bind us together in the name of Jesus Christ.

Bring encouragement, revelation, love, peace, and prosperity into your church. By the authority of the Holy Spirit, these things I declare and decree on behalf of all the people of God, in the awesome, mighty name of Jesus Christ. Father, in Jesus' name I use the mighty weapon of your Word to break the ties, and chains of bondage from over your people, for your Word shall not fail, in the name of Jesus Christ. Amen.

A Prayer Against Negativity

In Jesus' name, I cast down all imaginations of rejection, failure, worthlessness, and any thoughts that are contrary to your Word. I rebuke the spirit of fear that would try to torment me and I command it to flee in Jesus' name. I have been made righteous by your blood, Jesus, and I can do all things through you because you strengthen me and give me favour and wisdom. I choose not to think negatively or worry about what people think of me, but I will think about things that are good and praiseworthy. I will put into practice the things you have taught me, and I will follow your leading. I will fear no evil for you are with me. You go before me, Lord, and you are my rear guard. You comfort me when I am weak. Your plans for me are for good and not for calamity. I praise you, Lord, for your unfailing love and faithfulness. You are awesome Almighty God and I am humbled under your mighty hand. In your name I pray and give you thanks. Amen.

For Comfort

Glory Hallelujah, to our Lord God and Father. Blessed be God, even the Father of our Lord Jesus Christ, the Father of mercies, and the God of all comfort. Father God of all comfort, we come to you on behalf of all who are bereaved, whose loved ones have passed away. Covid, ill health, accidents and disasters have taken our loved ones. Comfort us, O God. Some have left us so suddenly, O God, so quickly and without warning, leaving us in shock and disbelief. We feel immobilised and struggle to deal with the grief. Father God, this grief and loss hurts so much; there is pain and sorrow, mixed with guilt and regret. And we know that you are acquainted with grief and understand our emotions and feelings of loss. And we pray, O God, attend unto our prayers, send your comforting spirit to heal our sorrows. Send your peace to guard our hearts and minds, mend broken hearts so that we might sleep and rest and be comforted. Hallelujah! Thank you Jesus. Comfort us in all our tribulation, that we may be able to comfort others in their grief, with thanksgiving and rejoicing. We give you thanks, Almighty God Jehovah. Amen.

Claim Healing

Father, guard us against life-limiting sickness and disease. Father, as hell is made for Satan and his angels, let sickness and disease be the same. Your Word says: "Who his own self bare our sins in his own body on the tree, that we, being dead to sins, should live unto righteousness: by whose stripes ye were healed" (1 Pt 2:24).

Father God, on the strength of your Word, we claim healing from our sins and from sickness unto death, in Jesus' name. Enable us, O God, to live righteously in your sight, that we might inherit eternal life through Christ Jesus. We ask and give you thanks, in Jesus' name. Amen.

Troubled By Troubles

Father, I come to you in times of trouble feeling like Job: battered, bruised and in trouble. Unlike Job, not knowing where to go or who to go to, I have tried to solve my problems with worldly solutions, not even seeing that the world is broken and that it will only have broken, temporary fixes. And now, Father, like the woman with the issue having spent all, I come to you seeking your face, Lord, and will accept the opportunity of touching your garment that I may be healed from all my troubles. Lord, have mercy on me, in Jesus' name. Amen.

Unclutter

Father, I pray you are well. Sometimes our lives become so cluttered with things that are of no use, but the problem is, like sin, they take up so much more space than the things we do use. And yet, Father, we don't rid ourselves of the useless things like sin in our lives and become laden with them, not able to run because of them, distracted by them. Father, can I have a big bin and a broom to pack and sweep them out my life. In Jesus' name. Amen.

CHAPTER 4

For Our Children
Looking to the Future

Introduction

Children are a heritage, a precious blessing from God. Abraham asked God for a son and God blessed Abraham and Sarah with Isaac in his old age (Gn 21:3). Hannah prayed to God for a son and was blessed with Samuel (1 Sm 1). He was the prophet who anointed David king. Through Scripture we can see God's plans for Isaac and Samuel being fulfilled. Similarly, God has good plans for our children (Jer 27:11). Jesus said, "suffer little children, and forbid them not, to come unto me: for of such is the kingdom of heaven" (Mt 19:14). Parents and other carers are responsible for ensuring that children know who Christ Jesus is. This responsibility includes teaching children to pray, understand Scripture and much more. The fruit of the Spirit: love, joy, peace, patience, kindness, goodness, faithfulness (Gal 5:22) are qualities that parents and carers must possess, teach and

43

demonstrate to children. According to an African proverb, 'it takes a village to raise a child'. And, in good Christian church communities, adult members have a godly responsibility to care for, protect and train children up in the way they should go (Prv 22:6). The prayers below give insight into areas where prayers are needed, and demand that we make intercession for all children without ceasing.

Children Our Blessing

Father in heaven, glory to your name. Your Word in Ps 127:3-5 tells us children are your heritage, and "happy is the man that hath his quiver full of them". Father, this leads me to make request for them to be protected from dangers seen and unseen. Father, put your Spirit in our children, call them, quicken their minds, make them teachable in school and at home, pluck them out bad company and out of every addictive habit. Father, in the name of Jesus Christ, watch them on the playground, in the park, keep them from peer pressure that causes negative behaviour and raise up wise parents, teachers and mentors to teach them in the way that they should go, in Jesus' name. Thank you Lord. Amen.

Salvation for Our Children

Lord, you promised in Acts 2:21: "And it shall come to pass, that whosoever should call on the name of the Lord shall be saved." And based on this promise, Lord, we ask you to save our children. Save them from sin and bring them under your protection. Your Word says in Jn 3:16:

"For God so loved the world, that he gave his only begotten son, that whosoever believeth in him should not perish, but have everlasting life".

Today, Lord, we come to you on behalf of our children and their children, our siblings, our relatives, aunts, uncles, grandparents and our Christian sisters and brothers in Christ. Lord, we pray that you would overshadow them in all their movements, sleeping, waking, walking, talking. Bless their speaking and listening Lord and open their ears to hear what you are saying, what you are speaking directly into their spirit. We pray that you would bless us with the words spoken in Ez 11:19: "And I will give them one heart, and I will put a new spirit within you; and I will take the stony heart out of their flesh and will give them a heart of flesh".

Lord, bring to pass in the lives of every father and every mother the words in Ez 36:27 that say: "And I will put my spirit within you, and cause you to walk in my statutes, and ye shall keep my judgements, and do them." In Jesus' name. Amen. Let the light and power of your mighty, everlasting Word transform their hearts and renew their minds. Cause them to run to you and cry to you each time they have an encounter with your holy Word, until they are surrendered to your Holy Spirit. Then let the miracle prophesied by Jl 2:28 become a now reality. Fill our sons and daughters with your Holy Spirit that they shall prophesy, give our old men dreams and our young men visions to help us grow closer to you, in Jesus' holy name. We thank you Father God. Amen.

For Rescue and Restoration from Brokenness

Father in heaven, great is thy faithfulness. Morning by morning new mercies I see. I thank you humbly in the name of Jesus Christ. Father, I come in the name of Jesus Christ on behalf of our children and parental relationships. Father, I ask you to restore broken parental relationships. Your Word says if any lack wisdom let him ask. Father, I ask you for wisdom to speak to, teach and lead our children in the way that they should go by your authority, as I plead the blood of Jesus to cover them. I pray for healing for our children's broken hearts, hurts and disappointments.

I pray for restoration from the problems of poor company, peer pressure, drug and alcohol abuse, physical, emotional and sexual abuse, anger, disobedience and stubbornness. Break the chains of disruption in them, break enemy strongholds that steal and destroy our children, "For all that is in the world, the lust of the flesh, and the lust of the eyes, and the pride of life, is not of the Father, but is of the world" (1 Jn 2:16). Lord, we ask you to break the pull of the world and set our children free. Help them to understand who you are and deliver them from the strangleholds of depression, suicidal thoughts and principalities, by the power and authority of the Holy Spirit, in Jesus' name. Amen.

Cover Our Children

Today, O Merciful God, we take up the authority given us, and in the name of Jesus Christ, we plead Holy Ghost protection over our children and their children's children, in the name of Jesus. We plead the blood of Jesus Christ to bind every demonic spirit sent to cause harm to our children. In Jesus' name, we command the spirit of torment to cease and leave our children now. By the power and authority of the Holy Ghost, we command every negative thought to cease their attack and leave our children's minds, leave their thoughts, leave their emotions, leave their personality, leave their peace, leave their relationships and every area of their young lives, in Jesus' holy name. We glorify your name, O God, Amen.

Guard Children's Hearts and Minds

Eternal Father of all Generations, we bless your holy name. Father, we pray for the generation of children being born in this time for covering under the blood of Jesus Christ. Father, stretch forth your hand, O God, and prevent the enemy from stealing and destroying our children. Guard their tender, impressionable minds, O God, speak into their hearts; call them, Lord, and cause their thoughts to be fixed on you. Let their desires be to serve you and give you praise all the day long, through Jesus Christ. Thank you Lord. Amen.

Awaken Parents

Father, awaken parents, and open their eyes to the dangers that surround, that entice and draw children into mischief. Pour out the spirit of blessed parenting upon mothers and fathers, guardians and carers to do supernatural work with children. Cause them to live righteously as godly examples. Give them wisdom, knowledge and understanding to train up each child in the way they should go to save them from sin. In Jesus' name, I give you thanks. Amen.

For the Unborn Child

Father God, Creator and Deliverer, I bless your worthy name. I call you today for the life of the unborn child. Lord God of heaven, babies are being aborted for reasons that we might not understand but you, O God, know all things. You are the creator of all life and every child belongs to you. Your Word says: But Jesus called them *unto him,* and said, "Suffer little children to come unto me, and forbid them not: for of such is the kingdom of God" (Lk 18:16). Father, as we pray, in Jesus' name, Lord, we ask you to speak life over these unborn babies and save them by your Holy Spirit. Thank you Lord, Amen and Amen.

For the Safety and Security of Little Girls and Young Women

Father God, all glory to your name. You alone deserve the glory and the praise. Today, Lord, I ask for help for all the girls and young women in the world. Father, help them to see themselves as you see them, to regard themselves as being fearfully and wonderfully made, not as objects to be used by boys and men. Father, I pray by the power of the Holy Spirit, for all who have experienced abuse. Heal the abuses, O God, send help, Lord, people they can trust – to lead them to you. Save them, O my God, they belong to you. Father, shield them from predators and rescue them from those who would sell them. Hallelujah! God, thou good and faithful God, hear us. All glory to your name. Amen.

A Calling for Boys and Young Men

Father, for every boy child and young man, I pray that according to your Word you would call them because they are strong. O Great Jehovah, too many are dying from the knife, the gun and the drugs. The gangs treat precious life as something disposable. I pray, Lord, for a great turning away from the life of sin and death, to a life of hope and eternal life in Christ Jesus. In Jesus' name, O God, cause every boy-child and young man across the world to hear your Word and turn to you. Worthy is your name, O Lord. Hallelujah, Amen.

For the Little Ones

Lord Jesus, you have told us in your Word: "suffer the little children to come unto me forbid them not for of such is the kingdom of heaven" (Mt 19:14). Lord, the enemy is waiting at the mouth of the womb to steal and destroy our children but your Word says, "it would be better for him to have a millstone tied around the neck and be thrown into the sea than for him to cause one of these little ones to sin" (Lk 17:2, NET). Lord Jesus, cover the little children. We pray under the power of your blood that every evil will pass by and not touch them. In Jesus' name. Amen.

CHAPTER 5

The Anointing Power for Service

Introduction

The anointing of God: what is it?

At the start of the early church, God anointed people with power for service and he still does today. This anointing was reserved for prophets, priests and kings; a type of inauguration into office, by the pouring on the head of oil or through the Holy Spirit coming directly to help that person. When a person is anointed to do work for God, the work is supernaturally accomplished. David was anointed three times (1 Sm 16:13, 2 Sm 2:4, 2 Sm 5:3). One of the many things David did was to play the harp to drive out the evil spirit and refresh the restless soul of Saul (1 Sm 17:14-23). Elijah was also anointed by God; he called down fire from heaven (2 Kgs 1:10). Finally, our Lord Jesus Christ was anointed by God to preach the gospel, and do many miracles in the Kingdom (Lk 4:18). It is the anointing of God, the indwelling and enabling power of the Holy Spirit that makes the difference. These prayers will help you gain a deeper understanding of the work of the Holy Spirit, seek His presence and His blessings in your life.

Anoint Us Lord

In the name of Jesus Christ, Father, you call the heaven and the earth and all that is in them. You created us in your image. Touch now our mouths to speak. I ask that you call leaders and set them over the nations and over the kingdom to root out and pull down, destroy and build, to instruct your people in righteousness, in the mighty name of Jesus Christ. Thank you Lord. Amen.

Paul and Silas Prayed

Father, your anointing set your disciples free. And at midnight Paul and Silas prayed, and sang praises unto God, and the prisoners heard them. And suddenly there was a great earthquake, so that the foundations of the prison were shaken, and immediately all the doors were opened, and everyone's bands were loosed. (Acts 16:25-34, KJV). Father, by your Holy Spirit, help us to pray earth-shaking, burden-lifting, soul-saving, delivering prayers. Thank you Lord, in Jesus' name. Amen.

Holy Spirit Power

Lord God of heaven, we honour your matchless name. You are God and there is none beside you. We ask that as we pray you will send your Holy Spirit to empower our words and bring them to pass. In the name of Jesus and by the power of the Holy Spirit which rose Christ from the dead, I declare every trial neutralised and brought to nought, and may that same Holy Spirit which has made us free from the law of sin and death (Rom 8:2) preserve you (Ps 121:8), lead you (Ps 27:11), teach you, and fashion you into His likeness. May the Holy Spirit help you, set you ablaze with the fire of God and reveal the deep things of God to you (1 Cor 2:10) for your good, in the name of Jesus Christ. Amen.

For the Child in the Womb

Holy Father God of heaven, Hallelujah to your name. Father God, I pray your anointing on the unborn child and upon your called-out ones, that they might fulfil every task in your plan for their lives and the lives of all who will come to you through the words that they speak, in the name of Jesus. Send healing anointing, O Lord, and send deliverance directly from your throne room, as we plea the blood of Jesus Christ over all. Glory to your name, Lord God. Amen.

There Is Power in the Blood

But if we walk in the light, as he is in the light, we have fellowship one with another, and the blood of Jesus Christ his Son cleanseth us from all sin (1 Jn 1:7). Having therefore, brethren, boldness to enter into the holiest by the blood of Jesus (Heb 10:19), and living way, which he hath consecrated for us, through the veil, that is to say, his flesh (Heb 10:20) let us utilise this privilege, in the name of Jesus to touch people's lives. Amen.

I plead the blood of Jesus Christ over and against every contrary condition and situation now and in the times to come. In the name of Jesus Christ, every sickness under the blood, every upset under the blood, every hurt under the blood and every demonic attack under the blood of Jesus Christ, I declare it. Let the backbone of sin be broken by the power of the blood of Jesus, and our sons, our daughters, mothers and fathers, husbands and wives, be covered under the blood of Jesus. May the miracle-working power of the blood of Jesus Christ continue to cleanse from sin by destroying every bondage and breaking every chain, in Jesus' name. Amen.

Life in the Spirit

I encourage us to be the proof of spiritual life. Human efforts and goodness without God, however valiant or sincere, can only poorly mimic the grace produced by the Holy Spirit. The difference between the self-righteous life without the Spirit and true spiritual living by the Spirit is like the difference between a Christmas tree and a fruit tree. We can hang fruit, and all kind of other things on a Christmas tree, but it bears no fruit. But a fruit tree bears fruit because it is the very nature of its life to do so. In the same way, the Holy Spirit within us will cause us to bear the fruit of the Spirit because this is the very nature of the spiritual life in Christ Jesus. Our response to the Holy Spirit should be to yield ourselves completely to His holy influences and direction. As we do, the harvest of the Spirit will be more and more evident in our lives.

My brethren, in the name of Jesus Christ, I pray that we will, by the power and authority of the Holy Spirit, produce fruit in abundance, in Jesus' precious name. Amen.

The Anointing Makes the Difference

Father, the anointing makes the difference. As Joseph was sold out to merchants, God, you had a plan for him. He was anointed to walk, anointed to be in Potiphar's household and anointed to resist a lustful woman. And even in the prison, the Bible says, "But the lord was with Joseph" (Gn 39:21), so that the plan in him would be fulfilled. Father, in the name of Jesus, anoint your people to resist temptation, that they may accomplish your will, in the name of Jesus Christ. Amen.

Samson's Anointing

Father God, in the name of Jesus, strengthen us Lord as you did your servant Samson and anointed him with the spirit of supernatural strength to defeat his enemies. He was in chains, enslaved and his eyes blinded. But through the power of your spirit that was upon him, he destroyed more of his enemies in his latter days than in the days before, that your name would be glorified, in Jesus' name. Amen.

The Power of the Blood

I declare by the power of the blood of Jesus, my Everlasting Saviour, that my soul is anchored to the cleft of the rock by the blood of Jesus Christ, and by his mercies my anchor holds. There is power in the blood, there is life in the blood; it kept the death angel at bay (Ex 12:13). For the life of the flesh is in the blood, and I have given it to you upon the altar to make an atonement for your souls, for it is the blood that maketh an atonement for the soul (Lv 17:11, KJV). The blood is redeeming, and almost all things are by the law purged with blood, and without shedding of blood is no remission (Heb 9:22). The blood has power to overcome the enemy (Rv 12:11).

I plead the prevailing blood of Jesus over you in every situation, over your family, over your ministry, against every attack of the enemy in the name of Jesus. Father, in the name of Jesus Christ, whosoever reads this prayer let them know that I plead the blood of your son Jesus Christ over them, and that they should plead the blood of Jesus Christ over someone else, in the mighty name of Jesus Christ that all might be saved. Amen.

Anointed in the Womb

Jesus and John were both anointed by God the Father before their birth. We know this because when Mary and Elizabeth met, the Spirit of God in them caused the babies to leap in their mothers' wombs. Father God, I pray for mothers to be anointed and their babies anointed as prophets, visionaries anointed with discernment, as lively stones, to build up and edify your church, to bring glory and honour to your name. In Jesus' name, I give you thanks and praise. Amen.

CHAPTER 6

Leadership – Church and World Leaders

Introduction

Proverbs 29:2 tells us, when the righteous are in authority, the people rejoice, but when the wicked beareth rule, the people mourn.

In countries where leaders rule cruelly or ineffectively, people live in fear and many in poverty. Human rights are not upheld. Where exactly are world leaders leading their constituents to? How fair or equitable is it to take food out of children's mouths, steal workers' pensions, and allow racist murders to continue? Young people are trying to show world leaders how wrong their leadership is, but they are not listening. They are not leading well. In the Apostle Paul's letter to Titus, he informs him of the qualities required of a bishop: someone who "must be blameless, as the steward of God ...", a person who holds firmly to the Word of God and preaches sound doctrine. He contrasts these qualities with the behaviours of the unruly, vain talkers and deceivers. World leaders could lead well if they followed godly principles, as all leaders must be blameless. Pray for them.

Feed the Flock of God

God is so very good to us. He has given us the good shepherd, who is Jesus Christ, His son, and He has also given shepherds to watch over and to encourage His flock. This is what Scripture says, "And I will give you shepherds after my own heart, who will feed you with knowledge and understanding" (Jer 3:15). Amen.

Our Father who art in heaven, holy is your name. Lord, I thank you for your righteousness, strength and wisdom. Lord, I know that you have called every single one of your children for a specific purpose and you have empowered them to walk in that purpose. Hallelujah!

Father, right now, I lift up true ministers of the gospel in Jesus' name. God, I thank you for the vision that you have given them for your church. I thank you that we are the church that you are building. I ask in Jesus' name that you send your Holy Spirit to cover, guide, and inspire your ministers. Give them strength, power, and understanding to teach your Word and to do so in a way that draws the unsaved to you. Lord, in Jesus' name, give peace and strength to your ministers and pastors. Amen.

Father, cause a refreshing new anointing to fill them, to move them ever forward by the power and authority of your Holy Spirit. Lord, give them clear direction and revelation about the building of your church. Protect them from those who would desire to harm and distract them. Give them spiritual discernment. Flow prophetically through them Lord, so that your Holy Spirit will dwell in them and the glory of God would manifest in their lives, in their relationships, and in the church where you are leading them. We give you thanks in Jesus' name. Amen.

Father, in heaven, I thank you that you alone are God. Glory hallelujah!

Lord Send Caring Shepherds

You are the God who gives life to the spiritually dead (Rom 4:17). I thank you that everyone who calls on the name of the Lord Jesus will be saved. But, how can these I'm praying for call on Jesus if they have not believed in Him? And how can they believe in Him if they've not heard about Him? And how can they hear without someone bringing the truth to them? And how can they hear unless that person is sent? (Rom 10:14-15).

Father, I ask you in Jesus' name to send someone into each of their lives, someone with the message of life, the Word of Christ, for your Word does not return empty; it accomplishes what you desire and achieves the purpose for which it is sent (Rom 10:17; Isaiah 55:11). May they hear the words of Christ, for His words are spirit and they are life. May the words that they hear not be stolen from their hearts (Jn 6:63; Lk 8:12). Lord, send good and caring shepherds who will speak your truth to your people, in Jesus' holy name. Amen.

Pray for Pastoral Leadership

Father, I thank you for your ordained true ministers. Thank you for protecting, strengthening, and overshadowing them. I pray in the name of Jesus for good health and length of days for pastoral leaders. I pray, O Lord, for your continued blessing on their lives and that no weapon formed against them shall prosper; they are your servants and your Word declares: touch not the Lord's anointed nor do his servants any harm. In Jesus' name, I pray that pastoral leaders would seek you for discernment, direction and leadership, not lean unto their own understanding, follow trends, traditions, personal agendas or anything that is not from the Holy Spirit and your Word.

I pray that they will discern and prioritise your righteousness, peace and unity as these are pleasing in your sight, O Lord. I pray for their determination and steadfastness in the gospel, in the name of Jesus, and that they should not be moved by the things of this world, rather that they would be unmovable and always grow in your grace, in the mighty name of Jesus Christ. Amen.

For Parliament

Glory to the name of our God. Hallelujah! Father, in the name of Jesus, I now directly pray into the houses of parliament for those who are responsible for making plans for the advancement of your people. Open their eyes, open their ears, pour out the spirit of compassion into them, cause them to exhibit mercy in their plans, in Jesus' name. Amen.

For Pastors and Ministers

Father, in Jesus' name, I come to you on behalf of ministers, pastors and leaders, asking that you re-anoint, refresh and strengthen them with the Holy Spirit and power to preach your Word. Father, I pray that they abound with blessings and that they do not grow weary in well-doing. Father, they are your creation created in Christ and equipped in every good thing to do your will; by the power of your Spirit, work in them that which is well pleasing in your sight. Father, by the power of your Spirit instruct them and teach them in the way that they should go, reveal the deeper things to them by your Spirit that they may be vessels of honour shepherding the flock willingly and eagerly and being an example to them and their own families, in Jesus' name. Amen.

In the name of Jesus, I lift up every pastor, minister and leader to you. Father, cover them with the blood of Jesus. Father, let the gifts and anointing on their lives come forth in Jesus' name. Open the eyes that are closed and birth the things that you have spoken to them in their hearts, as they continually give themselves to prayer and the ministry of your Word. In Jesus' holy name I give you praise. Amen.

For Pastors

Father God, glory to your holy name. By the power of the Holy Spirit I come to you in prayer for pastors that they would love you with all their hearts mind, soul and strength. I pray that they would experience the infilling and anointing of the Holy Spirit and honour Christ in their hearts, words and actions. I pray in Jesus' name that they would be loving, faithful, and Christ-like husbands to their wives. I pray that they would lead their families and the church with wisdom, courage and sensitivity that only Holy Spirit power can provide, that they may be empowered to abide in Christ and be devoted to prayer, relying on God. Amen.

By your power, Father, cause your ministers to rightly divide the Word of truth to every living person, communicating the gospel with clarity in Jesus' name. Cause those with hearts for the lost to increase in fruitfulness, and be effective in compelling the lost to Christ. Father, cover them, spiritually and supernaturally protect them from dangers seen and unseen as they work in integrity and obedience to your command in Jesus' name. Help them to create an atmosphere of unity and vision within the body of Christ and help them to discover new depths of understanding in your Word, in Jesus' name. Father, I pray that by your grace they will always experience good health, rest and refreshing from you and that they will demonstrate that grace, strength and compassion of Jesus towards all those that they lead in Jesus' name. Amen.

Teachers and Preachers

Father, in Jesus' name we ask you to send more Spirit-filled teachers and preachers into the midst of your church to speak the gospel and wisdom of heaven so that people will be emancipated from sin by your Word into a Spirit-filled life of righteousness and peace. Send your Word by your servants to heal and deliver your people in Jesus' name. Amen.

Lead Out of Chaos

Lord, the world is in chaos. There is nothing unaffected by the evil doings of evil people. Lord, you did not create a broken world; you said it was good when you made it, but the lack of good leaders has led to a world that is in rapid decline. Leaders have lost their way, taking a back seat in their role and putting undue stress on the people they are supposed to be leading. Lord, you are more than able; we look to you to send the leaders this world needs. Our eyes are upon you as we pray for anointed leaders who will make righteous decisions, in Jesus' name. Amen.

For Righteous Justice

Almighty, Everlasting Father, of all humankind, I give you praise. Lord, I pray for world leaders who will seek your face, who will deal righteously with isms, with racism and violence, protect the vulnerable, feed the poor and take care of the sick; leaders who will not leave the elders to die because they are old. I pray, Almighty God, do for the helpless. While the rich store up their riches, and poor live on the streets, Father God, I pray you raise up righteous, praying politicians to rule with equity and justice, in the name of Jesus Christ. Thank you Lord. Amen.

God Cover You and Keep You

I pray that God would bless and keep you, overflow you with peace, joy and all blessings from heavenly places. I pray in the name of Jesus that God would put your enemies to flight, that as they come against you one way they will flee seven ways by the blood and authority of the Lord Jesus Christ. Amen.

CHAPTER 7

Worship, Thanksgiving and Warfare

Introduction

Worship is an act of reverence, honour, to pay homage in thought and feelings or act to God. It is the act of bowing your heart, your head, lying prostrate, or falling before God with whom you have relationship and who is worthy of your worship and praise. Worship to God is an attitude, a way of being, saying from the heart, you are God and there is no one else like you. Worship to God is giving our very best, as did the Canaanite women (Mt 15:25): "Then came she and worshipped him, saying, Lord, help me". Worship is not all about singing. It is about worshipping God in spirit and in truth for the Father seeks such to serve Him. All of worship is all of Jesus Christ.

Who is Jesus Christ?

Jesus is the creator firstborn over all creation (Col 1:17), the creator of all things, the sustainer of all things, the head of the church, the one with all authority (Col 1:18). Jesus is the supreme message of all teaching, preaching and singing and should be the focus of all church activity. He is the resurrection (Jn 11:25), the firstborn of the dead (Rv 1:15), the conqueror of death who speaks to the dead raising them to life (Lk 7:14). He is the fullness of God (Col 1:19). He reconciles men to God (Col 1:20). He is the only begotten of the father (Jn 3:16), crucified died and rose again and sits on the right hand of God interceding for you and me (Mt 28:5).

He was broken for my brokenness, he is my peace with God, He is Lord, King, He is a way maker, He is the truth, He is the light (Jn 14:6), the bread of life (Jn 6:35) and bread of heaven (Jn 6:51). He is Emmanuel God with us (Mt 1:23). He is the Lord of lords and King of kings (Rv 17:14). He is God's offering, lamb of God (Jn 1:29). He is a shield and buckler (Ps 91:4). He is God our Saviour (Jude 1:25). He is closer than a brother (Prv 18:24). To him be glory throughout all the ages (Eph 3:21). Let Jesus Christ be Lord of your life today. Amen.

God bless you.

I Worship You Father

Father, glorious Father, I lift up your name. Your name exceeds all greatness. You are more than people can explain. Your beauty and splendour has us in awe. There is no match to your power and authority. I will stand and lift up my head to you and will kneel and bow my head to You. Blessed be, from glory to glory, your glorious exalted and everlasting name, in Jesus' name. Amen.

For Happiness and Rejoicing in the Spirit

I pray that this prayer brings happiness to your heart.

In the precious name of Jesus, I plea the blood from His side cover you and protect you from every assailant. In the name of Jesus, I command every unhelpful thought to leave your mind; by the power and authority of the Holy Ghost, may your thoughts be good, lovely, pure and edifying to your soul. In the name of Jesus, I command sadness and loneliness to flee from you, and your heart be filled with rejoicing in the Lord. Hallelujah! I pray that your children and your children's children's children's hearts melt at the hearing of the gospel of Jesus Christ, and as the deer pants for the water brook, they seek after the Word of Jehovah God all the days of their lives. In the name of Jesus, may the pains of loss and grief be lifted from you and the peace of God that passes knowledge saturate your being, raise you up with Holy Ghost power, in Jesus' name. Amen. Hallelujah!

Praise the Lord

(Ex 15:2): The Lord is my strength and song, and he is become my salvation: he is my God, and I will prepare him an habitation; my father's God, and I will exalt him.

(1 Pt 1:3): Blessed be the God and Father of our Lord Jesus Christ, which according to his abundant mercy hath begotten us again unto a lively hope by the resurrection of Jesus Christ from the dead.

(2 Sm 22:50): Therefore I will give thanks unto thee, O Lord, among the heathen, and I will sing praises unto thy name.

(1 Kgs 8:56): Blessed be the Lord, that hath given rest unto his people Israel, according to all that he promised: there hath not failed one word of all his good promise, which he promised by the hand of Moses his servant.

(1 Chr 16:8): Give thanks unto the Lord, call upon his name, make known his deeds among the people.

(1 Chr 16:9): Sing unto him, sing psalms unto him, talk ye of all his wondrous works.

(Ps 117:1): O praise the Lord, all ye nations: praise him, all ye people. In Jesus' name. Amen.

Adoration

Eternal God of hope and everlasting life, who gives strength, boldness and security to all that love you, I bring you adoration and praise. Let everything that breathes praise you, Lord. Let every person praise you. Like the hart pants for the water brook, my soul thirsts for you. One thing have I desired from you Lord and that's the one thing that I'm focused on, seeking for … You are the rock of my salvation and my joy. You lift my head above my enemies and cause them to scatter. Hallelujah!

There is no one like you who hears and answers prayers even before I have finished speaking, who keeps watch over me, guides me each day and keeps me from falling. My life is in your hands, in your plans. You know what I am thinking from a distance and see everything that I do. And, because you are my rock and my source of life, I can run safely through enemy lines without damage. Your word is a lamp to my feet and a light to my path. Thank you Lord. Amen.

A Prayer of Praise Unto Our Great God Jehovah

O praise the LORD, all ye nations: praise him, all ye people. For his merciful kindness is great toward us: and the truth of the LORD endureth for ever. Praise ye the LORD (Ps 117:1-2).

Come and hear, all ye that fear God, and I will declare what he hath done for my soul. I cried unto him with my mouth, and he was extolled with my tongue. If I regard iniquity in my heart, the Lord will not hear me: But verily God hath heard me; he hath attended to the voice of my prayer. Blessed be God, which hath not turned away my prayer, or his mercy from me (Ps 66:16-20). O that men would praise the LORD for his goodness, and for his wonderful works to the children of men! (Ps 107:8).

O most holy Father God, we honour your precious name. We thank you that when we were yet sinners, Christ died for us, that your mercy and kindness to us never ceases. We thank you for your integrity, for hearing and answering our prayers, forgiving us and taking us out of our mess. We thank you for your Word which tells us that nothing shall separate us from your love. And we thank you for the gift of the Holy Spirit and Jesus Christ our Saviour. Glory and honour be unto you our God, in the name of Jesus Christ. Amen.

Make a Joyful Noise

Father, we make a joyful noise to the glory and praise of your name. We lift up our hands and we acknowledge your greatness and all your goodness to the children of men. We declare that all people praise you: let the towns, country and nations bow before you in adoration. We thank you for being our God, fighting for us and giving us the victory. You are God and there is none else. Hosanna, Hosanna, Hosanna to the King of kings, in Jesus' name. Amen.

Against Evil Plans

Father, I give Your name glory, I lift up my hands in Jesus' name, and plea the everlasting blood of Jesus against every evil advance, principalities and powers. I ask you, Lord, in Jesus' name, turn every deception around and send them back to their places of origin. Father, rebuke the enemy, the accuser of your people, the father of lies, cause none of his evil plans to come to pass, dispatch angels from heaven to stop and spoil his evil enterprise, in Jesus' name. Amen.

I Love You God

Father God, I love you, you are my God, my eternal hope of salvation, from whom all my blessings flow. You fill my soul with gladness. Hallelujah! God of my life. Amen.

Victory

Give us help from trouble, for vain is the help of man. Through God we shall do valiantly, for he it is that shall tread down our enemies (Ps 60:11-12). But thanks be to God, which giveth us the victory through our Lord Jesus Christ (1 Cor 15:57).

Father God, I give you most holy thanks for deliverance and victories that you have secured for us over our adversaries, from dangers seen and unseen. I claim and declare victory over the enemy on every side in Jesus' name. I claim and declare victory over every affliction, over every sin, in the name of Jesus Christ. I claim and declare victory over every plan of the accuser of my soul, victory for my children, victory in Jesus' name, victory. Failure is not an option for me, because the Lord is on my side. The battle belongs to God, the victory belongs to God, in the name of Jesus Christ. By the authority and power given to me through Christ, I claim victory for my brethren and their families in the name of Jesus Christ. Amen.

CHAPTER 8

Guidance and Direction

Who can detect his own mistakes? Cleanse me from hidden sin (Ps 19:12, ISV).

Introduction

Many scriptures give us examples of how individuals received guidance and direction directly from God. In Acts 8, Philip was directed by an angel of the Lord to speak with a eunuch who was reading the Book of Isaiah. Philip preached Jesus to the eunuch, the eunuch said he believed that Jesus Christ was the Son of God and asked to be baptised. Without hesitation, Philip baptised him (Acts 8:26-39). Joshua, Solomon, Jehoshaphat, Deborah and Gideon and many more saints asked God for guidance and direction. Moses accepted the advice and guidance given by his father-in-law. You can ask God for guidance and direction rather than lean on our own understanding (Prv 3:5-7).

2 Chr 14:11

Then Asa called to the Lord his God, and said, "Lord, there is no one besides Thee to help in the battle between the powerful and those who have no strength; so help us, O Lord our God, for we trust in Thee, and in Thy name have come against this multitude. O Lord, Thou art our God; let not man prevail against thee."

Father, in Jesus' name for your church I pray, help us, for our children, our families, husbands, wives, help us, for the sick, those in hospital and in care, O Father help us. By your Holy Spirit-outstretched hand, and your divine power, when we are weak be our strength and help us, in Jesus' name, we ask and give you thanks, Lord. Amen.

A Prayer for Direction

Unto thee, O LORD, do I lift up my soul (Ps 25:1). Shew me thy ways, O LORD; teach me thy paths (Ps 25:4). Hold up my goings in thy paths, that my footsteps slip not (Ps 17:5). Lead me, O LORD, in thy righteousness because of mine enemies; make thy way straight before my face (Ps 5:8). Lead me in thy truth, and teach me: for thou art the God of my salvation; on thee do I wait all the day (Ps 25:5). My soul, wait thou only upon God; for my expectation is from him (Ps 62:5). You are my shepherd, my strength, my fortress, my strong tower, my balm, my healer and I put my trust in you alone. All glory to your precious name. Lord I worship you and give you praise, in Jesus' holy name. Amen and Amen and Hallelujah! Trust in him at all times; ye people, pour out your heart before him: God is a refuge for us. Selah (Ps 62:8). Hallelujah! Amen, Amen.

God's Strong Hand

Father, in heaven hallowed be thy name. I pray that your hand of grace and mercy will ever touch my friends, family, the church and the community. May your hand give spiritual guidance, direction and strength to us all in this time. I pray that your strong hand will uphold, defend and break strongholds, heal and deliver in the name of Jesus Christ. Father, may oils from the cup of salvation be poured out by your hand on your people, may your Spirit and your truth be in us, may the shadow of your wings cover us and hide us in your presence, in the name of Jesus Christ.

Father, fill us with a desire to serve you according to your will; fill us with Holy Spirit fire, help us with our spiritual armour and may the weapons of our warfare ever be in our hands to war and stand against the enemy of our souls, in Jesus' name. Overshadow your people, O God, with the spirit of discernment and wisdom that we may know the difference between right and wrong. Give us peace from strife, give us knowledge and understanding, as we seek a deeper and more meaningful relationship with you, and with each other. May your love cover us always, as I make these requests by faith, in the mighty name of our Everlasting Lord and Saviour Jesus Christ. Giving you thanks always, in Jesus' name. Amen.

Direct From Sin

Lord, blessed be thy name. When your only son was on the cross moments before He died, He prayed, "Father, forgive them for they know not what they do" (Lk 23:24). We need your forgiveness Lord. I make my request known to you now: cause all those who know that they have sinned and those who do not know that they have sinned to turn to you and be forgiven, in Jesus' mighty name. Amen.

Our Spiritual Weapons

Father God, we thank you for the strength and encouragement of your Word, which says: "For the weapons of our warfare are not carnal, but mighty through God to the pulling down of strong holds" (2 Cor 10:4). Hallelujah! "For we wrestle not against flesh and blood, but against principalities, against powers, against the rulers of the darkness of this world, against spiritual wickedness in high places" (Eph 6:12).

Father, in Jesus' name help us to understand that we are not fighting against flesh and blood, but against the enemy of our souls, the accuser of the brethren. Father, our enemies are not ordinary and there are many of them, needing extraordinary and supernatural weapons to fight and defeat them. Father, help us to grasp the power of your supernatural weapons, to have them always ready to defeat every plan of the enemy in Jesus' name. We pray for covering, Holy Spirit authority and power under the blood of Jesus that we will stand, be effective and victorious in prayer against every spiritual attack, in this time in this world, in Jesus' name, having put on the whole armour of God, praying always and watching in Jesus' name, Hallelujah! Father, we believe that your Word is true and we thank you for hearing and answering our prayers. We pray in the mighty, victorious name of Jesus Christ. Amen.

Peace for This Present Time

Father, in heaven, hallowed be thy name, from everlasting to everlasting, we bless You and praise you, Hallelujah, O God in Jesus' name. Thank you for today and for supplying all our needs according to your riches in glory – for waking us up to new mercies, nothing missing and nothing broken. We thank you, Lord, in Jesus' name. Amen.

Father, I humbly ask in faith and by the power and authority of Jesus' name, that you pour out your peace upon your people; the peace that is found in you that we might be still and know that you are God. I pray that we your children would be still and experience the enduring, Holy Spirit peace, the heavenly peace that Jesus left, a peace that the world cannot give; a peace strong enough to keep and guard us even in wartime, in perilous times. Grant us everlasting peace; a peace to end all conflict; a peace that unites. I pray for your peace to guard in sickness, for peace in lockdown, for peace to still the storms of life. Father, in Jesus' name, by the power of the Holy Spirit, cause your children to seek and find the peace that is created, by you, that is in you, that only you can give. In Jesus' holy name, I speak peace be still. Amen.

God Will Make a Way

As God was with Moses, walked with him, talked with him, hid him in the cleft of a rock and made a way for him, I pray in Jesus' name that in these troubled and trying times, through every trial, temptation and test, and through every supernaturally difficult situation, God will make a way for you and your family. Hallelujah! I pray for those who are sick, in the power and authority of Jesus' name, may our Lord be a balm for every pain: shoulder, back, knee and joint pain, headaches, and every medical problem. I pray that God would hide you in the secret of His tabernacle, and in so doing, cover every aspect of your life under the shadow of His wings, in Jesus' mighty name. Amen. Praise God, praise God, praise God!

Against Persecution

Father, in the name of Jesus Christ, I come to you praising and glorifying your holy matchless name. Hallelujah!

I pray in Jesus' name against the persecution of Christian brethren all over the world. Father, give them the right words, strong words, Holy Spirit-empowered words to speak boldly in whatever circumstances they find themselves. I pray that by the power of the Holy Spirit my brethren will understand and find strength and peace in the sufficiency of your grace even in their time of weakness, and I pray in the name of Jesus Christ, that those facing hardship would draw from the source, that you are to us all O God our Father. I pray and remember those imprisoned as though in prison with them and those who are ill-treated since I am also in the body. Father, have mercy on your servants. I pray for the love of the brethren to continue as we bear each other's burdens – that we may fulfil the law of Christ. I thank you Lord Jesus. Amen.

Jehoshaphat's Prayer

"And said, O LORD God of our fathers, art not thou God in heaven? And rulest not thou over all the kingdoms of the heathen? And in thine hand is there not power and might, so that none is able to withstand thee?" (2 Chr 20:6). "O our God, wilt thou not judge them? For we have no might against this great company that cometh against us; neither know we what to do: but our eyes are upon thee" (2 Chr 20:12).

How many times do we admit we don't know what to do and ask the Lord for help before we have a moan? Pray Jehoshaphat's prayer (2 Chr 20:6-12) out loud, making it your own as you pray.

Lord Jesus, Teach me

Lord Jesus, I ask you to intercede for me and teach me how to intercede on behalf of other people, so that your eternal blessings would flow throughout the nations, that every person who hears your Word and receives you as Lord would be saved. Thank you Lord. Amen.

CHAPTER 9

Your Spiritual Growth and Development

Introduction

To understand your place in the world, ask yourself this question: what is God's purpose for my life? God's plans and purpose for your life are for you to discover through daily prayer. As a child might ask their parent, ask Father God to show you what He wants you to do. In Acts chapter 9, Saul is zealously persecuting the church; he did not know God's plans for his life. It was not until he encountered Jesus in a most profound way that he began to understand God's purpose for his life. God changed Saul's name to Paul and anointed him to preach the gospel of Jesus Christ to the gentiles. Read and study the prophets' lives, see how God used them to instruct, warn and correct his people. Look at how Jesus' disciples grew through His teaching and follow His demonstration of godly living. Your spiritual growth and development is based on knowledge of God (Col 1:9-10). It is a spiritual journey of faith in the God whose Word is immutable; the Word that reveals the deep spiritual things of God. Grow in grace and in the unshakeable knowledge of God.

What Is My Purpose?

Father God, I pray that you would show me your purpose for my life so that I might live for you. Please keep me close to you, humbly learning and developing a deeper relationship with you. Don't allow me to go astray; help me to grow happily and develop the gifts and purpose you have placed in me. Father, in Jesus' name, I give you thanks. Amen.

Read and Study the Word of God

The Word of God is for our benefit and it is encouraging in every way. There is instruction, guidance and encouragement for our Christian walk with Christ Jesus; there are answers to life's issues and questions. The book of Colossians encourages thus:

"As ye have therefore received Christ Jesus the Lord, so walk ye in him: Rooted and built up in him, and stablished in the faith, as ye have been taught, abounding therein with thanksgiving. Beware lest any man spoil you through philosophy and vain deceit, after the tradition of men, after the rudiments of the world, and not after Christ. For in him dwelleth all the fullness of the Godhead bodily. And ye are complete in him, which is the head of all principality and power" (Col 2:6-10). Amen.

Be encouraged to read and study the Bible for yourself. Don't just accept everything you read or hear about the Bible or what it contains. When you read the Word of God, ask the Lord to give you a deeper understanding of his Word and draw you closer to Him. The Lord will speak to you through His Word. So, if you would like to know who God is, continue to read His Word – God's Word is true and reliable.

Keep on Praying

Prayer is a divine, spiritual activity and God is our sure trust – He never fails. Continue in prayer, don't give up – keep on praying. If you pray and feel that God hasn't heard you, pray again by faith believing that God has heard you. Believe the Word of God in 1 Jn 5:14. Pray and wait, be patient and give God time to do what He will, and to teach you the lessons you need to learn. The Bible says to be of good courage, to wait on the Lord and he shall strengthen your heart. It takes courage and faith to wait on the Lord to come through for us (Ps 27:14). When the Apostle Paul needed healing, he prayed three times to the Lord to heal him. The response from God was, "my grace is sufficient for you" (2 Cor 12:9). You must also listen to God's voice for His answer, because your answers exist in faith. Accept that God will not always heal as you might expect Him to, as healing is entirely in His mercy. And so with each prayer request, ask, believe and wait on Jesus. Amen.

1 Sm 23:9

When David faced the most difficult times, he would always turn to the Lord. David would often stop and enquire of the Lord for direction and wisdom. When we face difficulties, we too should stop and ask the Lord what we should do. Ask the Lord what you should do; the answer will come, if you will wait for it.

Isn't it strange how trouble can distract us from praying – using the most valuable weapon we have as Christians. Without prayer there is no help and no defence. David needed God's help and defence against King Saul.

Without prayer there is no breaking of chains, no subduing of the enemy, no breaking of strongholds, no overcoming evil, no victory, no healing, no restoration, no answers, no solutions. Why do so many of us find it hard to pray when we are in trouble? Is it because we don't have time to ask the Lord for help? Are we too busy trying to fix the problem ourselves or listening to the wrong kind of advice? Are we more capable than God, who says, I will be with you in trouble? God is not a man that he should lie: whatever He says He will do, He will do. Trust Him alone who is our trust. Call him. He says He will hear you and answer you. We must not lose our faith and trust in God to be who He is to us and for us.

I pray in the name of Jesus Christ that we would all gather up our strength, trust and faith in Christ Jesus, open our mouths and call Him in Jesus' name. Amen.

Stock Up On the Word

We remember you all in our prayers and we pray and desire that through prayer and the Word we should all come to the knowledge of the truth of our Lord and Saviour Jesus Christ. We therefore take on the responsibility of blowing the trumpet of God's holy Word. The Word tells us in Am 8:11: "Behold, the days come, saith the Lord God, that I will send a famine in the land, not a famine of bread, nor a thirst for water, but of hearing the words of the Lord." And so, my family, now is the time to turn to the Lord, repent, seek the Lord and live, seek good, and not evil that ye may live. Take some time to stock up on the Word of God, as hard times are coming.

Read the book of Amos, who came to tell the people about the Lord's intention because they transgressed His Word. Seek God, my friends, while He may be found. We will find Him now in His Word. His Word says, "Then said I, Lo, I come (in the volume of the book it is written of me,) to do thy will, O God" (Heb 10:7). We are living in a time where nothing else can fix the chaos in the world but the Word of God.

This, my friends, may be a hard but true saying, "The wages of sin is death, but the gift of God is eternal life" (Rom 6:23). It really doesn't matter who we are; this Word applies to us all. The Word of God is for our education and is written for us in love. Praise God. Praise God!

May God bless you richly, in Jesus' name. Amen.

Pray This Scripture

Greetings in the mighty name of Jesus Christ. My brethren, my encouragement to us today is to pray according to Eph 6:18, with all prayer, supplication, watchfulness and perseverance for all of us in the Spirit. Prayer in the Spirit is constant, without ceasing, varied, watchful, persevering, universal, and Bible-centred.

I pray that the spirit of prayer would rest on all of us today, assisting us when we do not know what to pray (Rom 8:26). I pray that the Spirit of God would bring forgiveness and repentance to the body of Christ. I pray in Jesus' name that the same Holy Spirit of God who rose Christ up from the dead would touch every deep-seated issue in our lives, even those to come. Bring life to every dead thing, every infirmity, release from every bondage, lead us into all truth, reveal to us things that are not of flesh and blood, in the mighty name of Jesus Christ. Thank you, Lord. Amen.

Lord Send Holy Spirit Anointing and Fill Me

O, Father of heaven and earth, send your Holy Spirit, the comforter, helper, revealer, leader into all truth, the Spirit of prayer to rest upon my soul. Fill my heart with the power of your Word, anoint me with your Holy Spirit, and daily draw me to the throne of grace! Help my infirmities, furnish me with strong, Christ-like, converting conversations, fire me with desire, impart faith, infuse power and authority through Christ Jesus. Enable me to ceaselessly continue in the prevailing preciousness and urgency of prayer, to be observant, awake and watchful in the same with thanksgiving, through Jesus Christ our Lord and Saviour. Thank you, Lord. Amen.

Spend More Time With God

Before the Holy Bible was translated from Greek, and the KJV was published and became publicly available, we didn't have personal-sized Bibles to read as and when we wanted to. Today the Word of God is not only available to us in printed form; we can access it electronically via different devices. The question is, how much time do we actually spend reading and studying our Bibles? Reading the Word of God is one of the ways in which you can spend time with God, along with prayer and worship.

The degree to which you get close to God depends on how much time you spend with Him. The closeness of your relationship with God will be seen in the ways you reflect His attributes in your daily life. So, make more time for God as you cannot make this faith walk without Him. When you spend time with God he reveals more of Himself to you, your faith increases, your relationship becomes stronger as you gain a deeper understanding of who God is, and your love for Him grows as you become more disciplined in your Bible reading, meditation, prayer and worship. Father God wants you to spend time with Him, He wants your time with Him to always be special, not rushed, so if you ask Him, He will grant your desire for a closer stronger relationship. He is waiting for you to call Him, so call Him today – don't delay. Be blessed in Jesus' name.

Eph 6:10, For Strength

Father, we give you praise. We lift you up, O thou most high. From the rising of the sun to the setting of the same, praises be unto your holy name. In the name of Jesus Christ, I pray for strength today; strength to be encouraged in the face of discouragement, strength to draw nearer, to become more confident and bold in my relationship with you. I pray for strength to serve you in these unprecedented times, and strength to call for help for all your people, in Jesus' name.

Father, I pray for words of strength, of faith and of life, that I might speak to strengthen and encourage your people and myself in Christ Jesus. Send your angels to minister strength to your servants as you did with Daniel. Father, give me strength to walk away from those who speak discouraging words – strengthen my love to pray for them. Your Word says I can do all things through Christ who strengthens me; fortify me, Lord, through your life-giving Word, for when I am weak you are my strength.

Father, you are my strength and shield, my source of resilience and my hope. And I know that through you I will fulfil my purpose. Father, I thank you for every victory that you have won on my behalf. In Jesus' precious name. Amen.

Declaration

Declare these words over your life. DECLARE OUT LOUD:

I am a child of the most high God, wonderfully and fearfully created, a treasure in earthen vessel, born in sin but by my Father's power delivered from sin. I stand victorious, an overcomer and a conqueror, filled with the power of the Holy Spirit. I am given my Father's words of power, authority, spirit and life to speak – life is in my tongue, I have healing for my body and my soul, I have access to my Father's throne room; Jesus Christ is my key, my defender, my mediator, my justification, my friend and my everything. I stand because Christ stands with me, in me – my life is hid with Christ in God, I have His shelter, His hiding place and strong tower. In Him I live, move, and have my being. I am a carrier of the peace Christ gave to me, bound by a charge to love, I have an abundance of grace and mercy for today, and God-given hope for tomorrow. Hallelujah!

My brethren, silver and gold I do not possess, but in the name of Jesus Christ, such things as I have and am in Christ, I bestow upon you ever more. In the mighty name of Jesus Christ our Lord forever. Amen.

Here Are a Few Key Scriptures to Guide Your Daily Prayers:

Mt 5:44 tells you to pray for the people who persecute you.

Be joyful in hope, patient in affliction, faithful in prayer (Rom 12:12).

Do not be anxious about anything, but in everything, by prayer and petition, with thanksgiving, present your requests to God (Phlm 4:6).

Devote yourselves to prayer, being watchful and thankful (Col 4:2).

Rejoice evermore. Pray without ceasing. In everything give thanks: for this is the will of God in Christ concerning you (1 Thes 5:16-18).

And pray in the Spirit on all occasions with all kinds of prayers and requests (Eph 6:18).

Lord Jesus, Still Be My Friend

I know a king; His name is Jesus. He instructs me to ask anything in His name and promises, according to His will, an answer. Lord, many of us have had an opportunity to ask anything in this life and have asked for riches that have not lasted. But, Lord, herein is my request: although I falter, would you continue to be my friend and my Lord, my rod and staff, my guide through this life, my help, my teacher and my shepherd? In your name. Amen.

CHAPTER 10

Encouragement to Keep Going,
to Press Onward

Introduction

The wonderful book Psalms expresses great encouragement to anyone who feels discouraged, sad, hurting and in need of support. Ps 34:6-7 was written by David when he pretended to be insane before Abimelech. "This poor man cried out, and the Lord heard and delivered him from all of his distress. The angel of the Lord surrounds those who fear him, and he delivers them" (ISV). You do not have to fake insanity to cry out to God; He will hear your heart's cry even if you don't speak out. Jesus sacrificed His life for you and the whole world. He said: "And remember, I am with you each and every day until the end of the age" (Mt 28:20, ISV). Do not allow life issues to hold you back; let go of the past and press onwards (Phil 3:13-14).

Don't Worry

The angel of the LORD encampeth round about them that fear him, and delivereth them (Ps 34:7). So, there is no need to worry; you are not alone. Moreover, what good can worry do for you? Jesus asked: 'And which of you with taking thought can add to his stature one cubit? If ye then be not able to do that thing which is least, why take ye thought for the rest?' (Lk 12:25-26). Casting all your care upon him; for he careth for you (1 Pt 5:7). Don't worry. Rejoice! Rejoice that God is with you. He has set up His camp and He will not leave you alone. God has not forgotten you. Talk with him today. Tell Him all your troubles. He cares for you and He loves you. Ask the Father for help, in Jesus' name. Let Him know how you feel and He will hear and answer you.

God, My Confidence – (Pray and believe what you pray)

Blessed be the name of the Lord God of heaven. My Father, he is Jehovah Jireh. Provide is what He does; He supplies all our needs out of His abundant riches in glory. He is Jehovah Shalom the God of his peace. His peace shall never be moved even in a world of chaos. He is a burden-bearer. He carries our load; it's never too heavy for Him, just cast them on Him. He is a way-maker; making a way out where there is no way is what he does. He is unstoppable, a defender of the weak, a shelter from the storm, a Father to the fatherless. In God My Father, there is no lack, no want, to them that love Him. In God there is joy unspeakable, good counsel, peace, freedom, protection, healing, a good job, a right position, right standing; since there is nothing made that was not made by Him, whatever you need, He can make it for you and for me.

My Father, God in heaven, tells us all where not to walk, stand, or sit, in order that He can bless us. He understands the language of the tears we cry; there is no one better to cry to. My Father God knows that doubt and fear will keep us from His blessings so He sent perfect love to evict them. Our Father knew we would have need of healing, so He sent His word to heal us. Our love for our Father provides an inheritance that prevents weapons formed from being victorious over us. God our Father makes all these blessings accessible through Christ to all by faith. Look at Rom 5:2. Not only that, but if it is in his Word, it is in his will. Read 1 Jn 5:14.

Brethren and friends, in the name of Jesus Christ by faith, confidence in God, His will, His Word, I pray and I receive the access given to every blessing, spiritual or temporal, not just for this generation, but every generation to come, may confidence in God and His will be added to you, in the mighty name of Jesus Christ. Amen.

Pray Even When You Don't Feel Like Praying

1 Thes 5:17 says, "Pray without ceasing." Here is a command without any modification. As long as people in any country, in any language, read the Bible, they will read this plain command to pray without ceasing. Pray in Jesus' name. Not only should we pray; we ought to pray all the

time! Prayer should be the continual turning of our hearts to God about everything (Phil 4:6). As a mother in her sleep listens for the cry of her baby, so too can our hearts be attuned to God listening for his voice, instructions and guidance while we're absorbed in daily duties or even while we're sleeping. Prayer should not stop even in our most difficult circumstances, as prayer works. Jesus prayed on the cross, the thief prayed on the cross, Paul and Silas prayed in prison. When we find it difficult to pray we can ask someone to pray with us and for us, because prayer works.

I pray that as we pray in the will of God, our answers will be granted in abundance, in the mighty name of Jesus Christ. Amen.

Read Joshua Chapter 9, 'The Gibeonite Deception', and Pray

Father God, we pray, that we, your servants, would be wise in our decision-making, that we would pray and seek your guidance before making decisions. We realise that at times we think we know exactly what to do but end up making mistakes. It is only then, when we are in trouble, that we take time to pray. Father, forgive us and deliver us from evil that thy will be done, in Jesus' name. Thank you, Lord. Amen.

I Plead the Blood of Christ

The words of a hymn by William Cowper 1772, say: "There is a fountain filled with blood, drawn from

Emmanuel's veins, and sinners plunged beneath that flood lose all their guilty stain". Father, glory to your name! In the name of Jesus and by the redeeming, Devil-defeating power of the blood, I come to you, seeking your face and your favour, Hallelujah! Hallelujah!

Father, I plead the blood that purchased and secured my peace with you, that way-making blood of Jesus Christ that opens doors. I plead the blood that washes, cleanses and purifies, the life-giving blood that heals, restores, and reconciles. I plead the blood of the Christ that protects over our children and your church. I plead the peace-giving blood of Jesus Christ over the lives of all my brethren, this city, this nation and the world.

I plead the riches of the priceless blood of Jesus Christ over all the families of the earth, for those who have not yet come, but will come by the power of the blood and the authority of Jesus Christ, Hallelujah! Hallelujah! I plead the wisdom, unity and love-giving power of the blood of Christ over our leaders in the church and in the world, in the mighty name of Jesus Christ. I plead the day-to-day strengthening power of the blood of Jesus Christ over every situation in our lives, so that death has to pass you by because the power of the blood of Christ is over you. I pray in the mighty name of Jesus Christ and say thank you Lord. Amen.

Peace Everywhere

Finally, brethren, rejoice, be made complete, be comforted, be like-minded, live in peace; and the God of love and peace will be with you (2 Cor 13:11). Be anxious for nothing, but in everything by prayer and supplication with thanksgiving let your requests be made known to God. And the peace of God, which surpasses all comprehension, will guard your hearts and your minds in Christ Jesus (Phil 4:6-7). For he is our peace, who made both one, and broke down the middle wall of separation (Eph 2:14). He makes peace in your borders; he satisfies you with the finest of the wheat (Ps 147:14).

In the name of Jesus Christ, I pray, where there are family issues, may the everlasting peace of God dissolve each unhealthy situation. If you are sick, in hospital or at home, may you experience the calming, healing balm of God's peace and His grace. Where conflicting attitudes and behaviours at work are affecting you, may the uncompromising peace of God reign in your soul, and your home be saturated by peace from above. Hallelujah! May your prayers be faith-filled, confident, effectual and fervent, bringing much reward. In Jesus' name, Hallelujah! Amen and Amen.

Pray Anyway

Daniel would rather spend a night in a den of lions than go without prayer for one single moment. All the king's leaders were against Daniel and they conspired to kill him because he prayed to his God. You won't always be liked, but pray anyway.

Read Daniel chapter 6 and pray.

PRAY IT NOW |**97**

Protection for Your House of Prayer

I pray that God protect you from the trap of foolish decisions and give you an unwavering heart. I pray that your house will be a house of prayer and that your household will serve the Lord, in the name of Jesus Christ. Amen.

Pray that (name's) house will be a house of prayer, allowing the Holy Spirit to lead you.

The Lord's Prayer

Pray the prayer that Jesus taught his disciples in Mt 6. Meditate on the words and pray your own inspired Holy Spirit prayer.

With God All Things Are Possible

Lord, God of heaven, we lift you up as the most high and unto your great name sing Hallelujah praises in Jesus' name. I pray for the Spirit-filled preaching of the pure word of truth and for anointed ministers to do the same. I pray for a people of integrity, men and women who are filled with the Holy Spirit, strong leaders with sound, godly principles who will stand in the face of adversity in Jesus' name. Hallelujah, Hallelujah! Father, I pray in Jesus' name, that the power of salvation would knock on the door of every unsaved heart in Jesus' name. Amen.

Father, I pray for an outbreak of repentance, forgiveness and peace in your people; a peace that would pour out and into this community, nation and world. I pray for an abundance of love and fellowship to do the same. I pray for deliverance and breakthrough by the blood and power of Jesus' name. I pray for restoration, strength, healing and the breaking of every curse in Jesus' name. I pray in the name of His Lordship, Jesus Christ, that as you dwell in the secret place of the Most High, no plague, pestilence, no fire or flood shall come near your dwelling. I pray for all our families, especially for the children, to be under divine protection of the Most High God.

I pray for holy, lifted hands doing righteousness, anointed lips speaking and stopping every wicked plan of the enemy in the name of Jesus Christ. I pray for every need supplied, every brokenness be made whole. I pray, Lord, cause the weak to declare "I am strong," and the poor to declare "I am rich," in Jesus' name. I pray for a balm for every pain, I pray for encouragement against every criticism, the turning around of every lie for a blessing. I pray that every situation that looks like a failure be made a celebration of prosperity, for there is no failure in God. Father, in heaven, with you all things are possible and that is why I make these requests by faith, in the name of Jesus Christ, the son of the living God. Lord God of heaven, I thank you in advance. Amen.

ABOUT THE AUTHORS

Barrington L Moore is a semi-retired, skilled motor vehicle engineer, a former highly commended AA patrolman, former NVQ trainer in motor vehicle maintenance skills. Barry has worked for several large motor vehicle dealerships, delivered advice to garages and made representation on their behalf in MOT standards dispute cases. He is a former logistics planner and delivery driver. Barry has contributed many skills and hours to local churches as a volunteer: teacher of adult Sunday school alongside his mentor and friend pastor Adrian Cox, preacher of the Word of God, street pastor, health and safety team, men's ministries, prison ministries visitor, BtG and prisoner resettlement support, regional prayer co-ordinator – leading prayers. Barry is responsible for starting PrayItNow Ministries through the leading of the Holy Spirit.

Valerie M Moore is former assistant director of student services at the Open University. She has worked extensively in education and training. She is former senior lecturer at Manchester College. Valerie's academic experience combines PhD research projects, Joseph Rowntree research fieldwork, contributions to educational publications, including 'Black Families in Britain as the site of the struggle'.

Valerie is co-founder of the Afrikan Curriculum Development Association, which she chaired for many years. She is an experienced generic advocate and mediator. Valerie has volunteered at local churches as: assistant Sunday school superintendent, children's teacher, street pastor, prison visitor and women's ministries and cleaning team member. Valerie is mother to Julian and Matthew and grandmother to Evelyn Jane and Liliana Isobel Blake. Through Holy Spirit guidance, Valerie writes prayers and encouragements and leads prayers alongside Barry in PrayItNow Ministries.

Author email address and website:
office@prayitnowministries.org.uk
www.prayitnowministries.org.uk

www.marciampublishing.com

www.ingramcontent.com/pod-product-compliance
Lightning Source LLC
La Vergne TN
LVHW051658080426
835511LV00017B/2623